NATURE'S MYSTERIES

By Nancy Vogel

Modern Curriculum Press
Parsippany, New Jersey

Credits

Photos: All photos © Pearson Learning unless otherwise noted.
Front Cover: Bruce Davidson/Animals Animals. Title page: ©Lawrence Naylor/Photo Researchers, Inc. 5: C.C. Lockwood/Bruce Coleman, Inc. 7: Corbis-Bettmann. 9: James L. Amos/Corbis. 10: Brandon D. Cole/Corbis. 11: International Society of Cryptozoology. 14: Corbis-Bettman. 15: The Granger Collection. 17: Reuters Newsmedia, Inc./Corbis-Bettmann. 18: ©C.E. Mohr/Photo Researchers, Inc. 20: Catherine Karnow/Corbis. 21: Charles Tait/Ancient Art and Architecture Collection. 23: Corbis/Bettmann. 25: AP/Wide World Photos. 26: Robert H. Rines/Academy of Applied Science. 28: Corbis-Bettmann. 30: International Society of Cryptozoology. 33, 35: UPI/Corbis-Bettmann. 36: Rene Dahinden/Fortean Picture Library. 38: Hulton-Deutsch Collection/Corbis. 39: ©Lawrence Naylor/Photo Researchers, Inc. 41: David Hulse/World Wildlife Fund. 43: Roger Ressmeyer/Corbis. 44: Ralph White/Corbis. 45: ©Tom McHugh/Photo Researchers, Inc. 46: Wolfgang Kaehler/Corbis

Illustrations: 20, 29, 35, 39, 41: Mapping Specialists, Ltd.

Cover and book design by John Maddalone

Modern Curriculum Press
An imprint of Pearson Learning
299 Jefferson Road, P.O. Box 480
Parsippany, NJ 07054–0480

www.pearsonlearning.com

1-800-321-3106

ISBN 0-7652-2162-4

2 3 4 5 6 7 8 9 10 11   MA   07 06 05 04 03 02 01

Modern
Curriculum
Press

Contents

To children who like stories
of the strange and mysterious: May you find
wonder in the world.

Hidden Animals

Did you know that some people think a dinosaur lives in a lake in Scotland? Other people say they have seen a huge, humanlike animal in the mountains in California.

Ever since ancient times, people have been trying to solve the world's mysteries. They have climbed mountains, explored forests, and gone deep into the oceans. They have studied and tried to explain everything they've seen.

Biologists gather and study turtle eggs.

Although much has been explored and studied, there is still a lot to discover. Scientists have not yet studied every kind of animal and plant that lives on Earth. Believe it or not, scientists are discovering new kinds of plants and animals all the time.

There are many animals that scientists have heard about but haven't been able to find in order to study them. These are the hidden animals. If you are thinking that a hidden animal sounds like an animal that is playing hide and seek, you are almost right. When scientists talk about hidden animals, they are talking about animals that are unknown or hidden from science. These animals exist even if no one has actually seen them or proven their existence.

The scientists that look for and discover new animals are called *cryptozoologists*. This word combines three Greek words. They are *kryptos* (hidden), *zoo* (animal), and *logos* (discussion). So *cryptozoology* is the scientific discussion or study of hidden animals. This makes cryptozoologists scientists who study hidden animals.

The animals that cryptozoologists search for are called *cryptids*. A cryptozoologist's job is to gather evidence on cryptids and study it. After scientists gather evidence and identify a mysterious animal, it is not a cryptid anymore. Only hidden, mysterious, and unknown animals are cryptids.

Of course, the animals that cryptozoologists discover are not really new. They have been there all along. They simply were not widely known and not classified by science. No one has been able to get close enough to decide what kinds of animals they are.

Scientists excavate buried dinosaur bones.

Scientists classify, or organize, animals into groups, such as mammals and reptiles. Among the different classifications are smaller subgroups. These may be meat eaters and plant eaters, or creatures that crawl and creatures that fly. For example, a wolf is a mammal. It is also a meat eater.

Cryptozoologists have many ways to search for a hidden animal. Sometimes they follow stories. They listen to people describe an animal they claim to have seen. The animal may not match the descriptions of any known animal. If many people say they have seen the animal, scientists may decide to investigate. They will look for the animal themselves to see if it really exists.

If scientists are very lucky, they may have more than just eyewitness reports to go on. There may be physical evidence, too. Examples of physical evidence might be footprints, hair, skin, feathers, bones, or body parts of an animal that has died. It's easier for scientists to figure out the truth if they have more evidence to study.

In some cases, cryptozoologists have proved that an animal still exists that was long believed to be extinct, or gone from the earth. When this happens, the discovery is called a living fossil.

A fossil is any part of a plant or an animal that lived long ago that has hardened and is found in rocks. An animal fossil might be a bone or a tooth. It could be a footprint or an outline of a body that was pressed into mud that turned into rock over thousands of years. Of course, a living fossil isn't really a fossil at all. It's a living animal that matches fossil remains found by scientists.

Fossil imprint of an ancient fish

A manatee

In other cases, cryptozoologists have found animals that no one had seen or heard of before. Sometimes creatures that were long thought to have been only stories, like the manatee, are found to be real. Some scientists believe that the manatee is behind reports of mermaid sightings. Viewed through water, this mammal can look like a human body with a finlike tail instead of legs. The real creature turned out to be more ordinary than the story's version. It was also an animal that was not correctly identified in the past.

Sometimes there is a simple explanation for what seems to be an extraordinary creature. Sometimes there isn't. This is what makes cryptozoology such an exciting science.

Cryptozoology became a real science in the 1950s through the work of a French scientist named Bernard Heuvelmans. When he was a boy, Heuvelmans liked to read about strange creatures. When he grew up, he studied real animals and became a zoologist.

As a scientist, Heuvelmans was still interested in strange and unusual animals. He wondered if the stories people told about mysterious animals might really be true. He decided to gather all the material he could.

Dr. Bernard Heuvelmans

11

Heuvelmans put together stories, investigations, and evidence people had collected. Then he compared the facts and reports with what he learned about known animals of the same type.

In just a few years, Heuvelmans had collected a lot of information about mysterious animals. He was able to write a book called *On the Track of Unknown Animals*.

Scientists respected the book because of the careful research that went into it. People who were not scientists enjoyed reading about these mysterious animals. The book became very popular around the world.

As he continued his research and writing, Heuvelmans decided that he needed a new word to describe what he was doing. So he invented the word *cryptozoology*.

Heuvelmans not only gathered information he had read, but also traveled to meet people who had seen mysterious animals. He also traveled all over the world to look at physical evidence that people had found. Then he wrote a second book about cryptids in the oceans. It is called *In the Wake of the Sea-Serpents*.

For years some scientists made fun of cryptozoologists and their interest in hidden animals. These scientists did not believe there were any unknown animals. Again and again the cryptozoologists have proved those who doubted them to be wrong.

Hidden Fact

The International Society of Cryptozoology was founded in 1982 at the Smithsonian Institution in Washington, D.C. Bernard Heuvelmans was elected president. The group defined cryptozoology as the study of "unexpected animals."

Chapter

The Kraken

One of the earliest cryptids to be proven real was a sea monster that was called the kraken (KRAH kun). Reports of this huge sea monster go back hundreds of years. They begin with an account of such an animal stranded on a beach in Iceland in 1639. Stories about an enormous sea creature with large and very long tentacles, or arms, were also told in Ireland and Norway. The kraken turned out to be a giant squid.

An engraving of the kraken and a three-masted ship in rough seas

In 1861 the crew of the French ship *Alecton* spotted what looked like a gigantic sea monster off the coast of Africa. The sailors tried to capture it, but the creature swam away. The *Alecton* sailed after it. After a long chase, the sailors finally got close enough to try again.

This time the crew tried to catch the creature with a harpoon. A harpoon is a kind of long spear attached to a rope. It has a large, barbed hook at one end. The sailors managed to spear the creature. Then they tied a rope around its body and tried to haul it onto their ship. The rope slipped. The body of the sea monster fell back into the sea. Only a small part of the tail was saved.

An engraving of sailors on the *Alecton* harpooning a giant sea monster

15

The captain of the *Alecton* reported what had happened as soon as his ship reached land. The captain's official report was later presented at a meeting of the French Academy of Sciences. The Academy made fun of the story. They said the creature could not possibly exist. No one believed that the sailors on board the *Alecton* were telling the truth.

A Danish zoologist named Johan Steenstrup had no better luck. He researched the same creature and published a description of it in 1857. He even collected pieces from fishermen who had captured the creatures. Even with the evidence, no one believed his stories of a giant squid.

Finally, in the 1870s, a number of creatures that matched the description of the kraken washed up on shores in Canada. Now there were actual remains of a whole creature to study. A group of scientists went to Canada to investigate.

In 1873 a fisherman and his son found a giant squid near Newfoundland. They chopped off a piece of one tentacle, which measured 25 feet. They said they had left 10 feet of the tentacle on the creature. They brought the piece of tentacle back on their boat and showed it to an investigator. He claimed the whole animal must have been about 60 feet long and 5 to 10 feet wide.

These findings led more scientists to take the reports seriously. They wanted to study this amazing sea creature. They finally decided it was a giant squid after comparing the pieces that had been found with other similar animals. Until then, scientists simply did not accept the fact that squid could grow to such an enormous size. Now scientists know that they can.

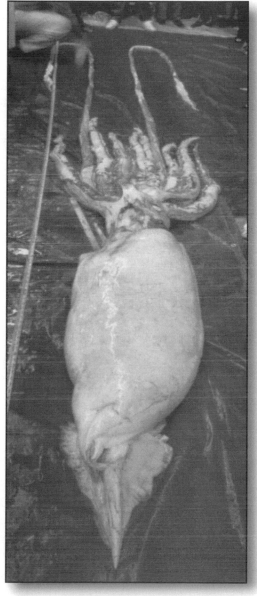

A giant squid

Suckers on a squid's tentacle

Squid are a kind of sea creature known as a bottom-feeder. This means that the animal usually stays near the bottom of the ocean. This is why people rarely see giant squid.

Learning about giant squid has cleared up at least one mystery in nature. Strange round marks found on some whales used to puzzle scientists. Now they know that these are sucker scars. They were made by giant squid in battles with whales.

The suckers are round pads surrounded by sharp teethlike points on the underside of the tentacles. They help the squid's tentacles hold onto animals the squid is trying to fight with or wants to eat.

The marks on the whales were where a squid had grabbed them with its tentacles and held onto them with its suckers. Some fishermen have reported seeing battles between a huge whale and a giant squid. Because the scientists had not believed that squid grew so large, they had not connected the enormous round marks with squid suckers.

Oceans are so big and deep that it's not surprising that some animals living there have remained hidden. It may seem easier to find a hidden water animal in a lake, but that is not always the case.

Hidden Fact

How big can a giant squid get? The largest specimen scientists have examined was found in New Zealand in 1880. It measured 65 feet, of which 30 to 35 feet were its tentacles. Other eyewitnesses have reported seeing giant squid as long as 90 feet!

Chapter 3

The Loch Ness Monster

One of the most famous cryptids is the Loch Ness Monster. The word *loch* is Scottish for "lake." Loch Ness is a large lake in the northern part of Scotland. It is about 20 miles long and about one-and-a-half miles wide. Hundreds of people claim to have seen a strange creature in the lake. Stories about this creature go back over 1,500 years.

Loch Ness

A carving from long ago that could be a sea monster in Loch Ness

Ancient carvings on rocks in the Loch Ness area show a strange creature with a long snout and four legs that end in flippers. Some people have described it as looking like a swimming elephant. They think that the creature's very long snout, or nose, looks like an elephant's trunk. Some people believe that these carvings record a strange creature that people saw in the lake long ago.

Until 1933 the descriptions that people had given of the creature were thought to be only stories. Then in 1933, a road was built that ran along the shore of the lake. People who began driving on this road suddenly had clear views of the lake.

As more people traveled around Loch Ness, they reported seeing a strange creature in the lake. Some took pictures of it. However, when the film was developed the pictures were too blurry to show anything clearly. Still, people liked the idea of a mysterious creature living in Loch Ness. The creature was even given the nickname Nessie.

Most people described the lake monster as being very large. They said it was the size of a small boat, with one or more humps along its back. Many people saw what they thought were a long neck and flippers. Its movement was wavy as its flippers pushed it this way and that in the water. One couple said they watched an "enormous animal rolling and plunging" in the water.

Many scientists said it was impossible for such a creature to exist in the lake. There was no real proof of its existence. They said what people had really seen were logs, boats, or other ordinary things.

Other scientists disagreed. They thought it was possible that a prehistoric creature from the time of the dinosaurs might have been able to survive in Loch Ness. Because the loch is 900 to 1,000 feet deep, it made a good hiding place.

Drawing of a plesiosaur

These scientists examined all the known creatures. The plesiosaur (PLEE see uh sawr) was a likely match. Plesiosaurs were a kind of reptile. They were known to exist in the Loch Ness area in large numbers at the time of the dinosaurs. They had long necks, small heads, and four diamond-shaped flippers. Their bodies were 20 to 40 feet long. However, plesiosaurs are believed to have been extinct for at least 65 million years.

Other cryptozoologists thought the creature could be a zeuglodon (ZOO gluh dahn). Zeuglodons were similar to whales but with much longer and thinner bodies. Zeuglodons were believed also to have been extinct for 20 million years.

Only one thing was known for sure. Nessie sightings increased. Some turned out to be hoaxes. These were jokes that people tried to play. Many sightings were from honest people, though. Whatever the creature turned out to be, these people were convinced they really did see something unusual in the loch.

There were so many reports that in 1957, a local doctor named Constance Whyte decided to write a book about them. She believed honest people should not be made fun of because they told the truth about what they saw.

Dr. Whyte spent years collecting stories from everyone who claimed to have seen Nessie. She thought that a book detailing these eyewitness accounts could somehow make the stories more believable. She called the book *More Than a Legend*. It had so many details of Nessie sightings by so many different people that scientists finally began to pay attention.

Scientists planned four separate expeditions to explore the loch. They decided to use a new technology called sonar. Sonar works with sound to find objects underwater. Sound waves are sent through the water. If they hit an object, they bounce off it and back to a machine that records them. The record of the sound waves shows the shape of an object. Each time the sonar was used in Loch Ness it found large objects moving underwater. No one could explain the objects.

This famous photograph of Nessie has since been proven to be fake.

All this proved was that there was something in the loch. It didn't prove that it was anything extraordinary. Then a new expedition was launched in 1975 to find Nessie.

The new expedition used a special kind of sonar along with underwater photography. A bright light flashed and a picture was taken every 45 seconds. One night the scientists finally discovered something interesting.

At the same time the sonar showed a large object moving underwater, the underwater camera took pictures. In the pictures was an object that looked like the flippers of a swimming creature. This new evidence was presented before the British government. Sir Peter Scott, a well-known scientist, said the puzzle of the Loch Ness was solved. He believed Nessie was a plesiosaur or a family of plesiosaurs. He said they were not extinct as scientists had thought.

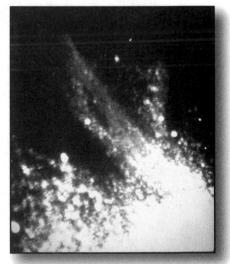

This photo taken with sonar in 1975 may show Nessie's flippers.

Not everyone believed this idea. The photograph that had been taken underwater was very dark and hard to see clearly. Though many more expeditions have searched the lake over the years, no one has yet come up with proof that Nessie really exists at all. So the general belief is that no one can say for sure if there is a Nessie or what kind of creature Nessie might be.

Cryptozoologists continue to study Loch Ness. If Nessie does turn out to be a plesiosaur, it will be a fascinating discovery. It will also be proof that cryptozoology truly can discover modern marvels.

Hidden Fact

In the 1930s, people were so interested in Nessie that a circus offered a big reward for Nessie's capture. The quiet and lonely lake at Loch Ness became crowded with sightseers. Hundreds of people set out in small boats, hoping to claim the prize money.

Chapter

A Living Fossil

If the Loch Ness monster was discovered and proven to be a plesiosaur, it would be an example of a living fossil. Remember that living fossils are animals thought to be extinct that cryptozoologists or others discover are actually alive. One of these living fossils is the coelacanth (SEEL uh kanth).

A model of a coelacanth

The coelacanth has a bright blue or sometimes brown body that can grow up to five feet long. Coelacanth fossils have often been found in the rocks of lakes and oceans. That's why scientists believed it had been extinct for 65 million years.

In 1938, the coelacanth became more than a long-dead fossil. A fishing ship sailing near the coast of South Africa found an unusual fish in its net. The fish was five feet long, with large, bright blue scales.

Marjorie Courtenay-Latimer worked at a local museum. She was interested in any unusual fish that local fishermen caught. The captain of the fishing ship called her about the bright blue fish.

When she saw the fish, Courtenay-Latimer described it as the most beautiful fish she had ever seen. She said it was five feet long and was a pale purple-blue with shiny silver markings.

However, by the time she saw the fish, it had been out of the water for some time. It was beginning to smell very fishy. She wanted to take it back to the museum, but she had trouble getting a taxi driver to let her put the smelly bundle into his car.

Marjorie Courtenay-Latimer stands behind the first coelacanth ever found.

Courtenay-Latimer sent a message to a leading ichthyologist, a scientist who specialized in the study of fish. He was away. Marjorie couldn't wait for him. The fish was getting older and smellier all the time.

When she didn't hear back from the scientist, Professor J.L.B. Smith, she made a detailed sketch of the fish. Then she gave the fish to a taxidermist so it could be stuffed and preserved.

When Professor Smith finally saw the sketch, he couldn't wait to examine the fish. By the time he got to South Africa, it was too late. All the fish's insides, including its skeleton and organs, had been thrown away. All that was left was the preserved outside of the fish.

Professor Smith immediately identified the preserved fish as a coelacanth. It was a discovery he had been expecting. "I always knew somewhere or somehow, a primitive fish of this nature would appear," he is reported to have said.

As a living fossil, the coelacanth was a very important zoological find. With only the skin preserved, many questions were left unanswered. Scientists needed to find another coelacanth. They needed a fresh, whole fish so they could prove that it really was a coelacanth.

Professor Smith went up and down the East African coast. He posted a notice with a picture of the fish and offered a reward to any fisherman who caught one and brought it to him. Then he waited.

It took almost 15 years. Finally another coelacanth was caught in the Comoro Islands. The islands are between southeastern Africa and the large island of Madagascar. Professor Smith lost no time in flying there. When he saw the dead fish, he cried. He had waited a long time to prove that a fish like the coelacanth really did exist.

Since then, hundreds of coelacanths have been caught and studied. Many cryptozoologists now ask, if the coelacanth can survive on our planet for 65 million years, why couldn't a plesiosaur do the same in Loch Ness?

Hidden Fact

Some coelacanths were discovered living in deep caves along the sides of underwater volcanoes. Cryptozoologists believe that they now know in what kinds of places to look. They hope they will soon find even more coelacanths.

Bigfoot

Bigfoot is probably the most famous cryptid in North America. Almost everyone has heard of Bigfoot. Thousands of people all over the United States and Canada claim to have seen this creature. Native Americans have stories about Bigfoot, or Sasquatch, that go back for hundreds of years. Movies have even been made about Bigfoot.

An artist's drawing of what some people believe Bigfoot looks like

Not everyone agrees on all the details of Bigfoot's appearance. Most sightings do have a few things in common. Bigfoot is usually described as very tall, from 7 to 10 feet in height. The creature is covered from head to foot with long, shaggy brown hair. It is able to move very quickly with large strides. Another thing people have said is that Bigfoot smells bad, like a person who hasn't bathed in a long time.

Other, less common details are that it has a big chest, a small head that is somewhat pointed, and no neck or forehead. Some people say that Bigfoot travels alone. Others claim to have seen family groups. Some say they have even heard Bigfoot scream and howl.

Of course, Bigfoot's most well-known feature is described in its name. Whenever people claim to have found footprints of Bigfoot, the prints are always huge. Tracks found in 1958 near Bluff Creek, California, measured 16 inches long and 7 inches wide. That is a big foot.

Many people don't believe that Bigfoot is real. They think it is really a bear or another ordinary creature. Many of those who do believe Bigfoot is real have spent their lives tracking this creature. One person who looked for Bigfoot for many years was Roger Patterson.

In October of 1967, Patterson and a friend named Bob Gimlin were riding on horseback in Northern California. They'd been camping in the woods. They were using a motion-picture camera to shoot film Patterson hoped to use in a movie he wanted to make about his search for Bigfoot.

A photo of what may be Bigfoot taken with Roger Patterson's motion-picture camera

Suddenly, they saw something. Walking into the woods ahead of them was Bigfoot! Then Roger's horse smelled the creature and reared up. The horse stood so high on its back legs, it toppled over. Both horse and rider fell to the ground.

Roger quickly got up, found his camera, and shot all the film that was left. He recorded the creature from three different angles. His friend, Bob, stayed on his horse, ready to help in case the creature attacked Roger.

After Roger shared his incredible film with others, Bigfoot investigators rushed to the site. A man named Bob Titmus found footprints that seemed to match the path taken by the creature in Roger's film. He made plaster casts of ten of them. Everyone wondered if this finally proved that Bigfoot was real.

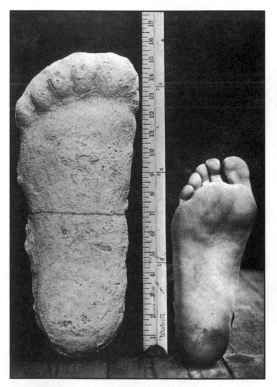

A plaster cast of Bigfoot's foot compared with a human's foot

The Patterson film is still talked about to this day. Some people claim it is proof that Bigfoot exists. Others claim the film is a hoax, or a fake. They think that the image in the film is nothing more than a man wearing a shaggy suit.

Roger Patterson died in 1972. He always swore that his film was real. Researchers and cryptozoologists continue to investigate Bigfoot sightings. As of yet, they have not found positive proof, such as a living Bigfoot held captive or even a skeleton.

Hidden Fact

All over the world, people tell stories about wild creatures like Bigfoot. In Australia this creature is called the Yowie. In Tibet it is called a Yeti. Whatever it is called, Bigfoot sightings continue to this day. They now number well into the thousands.

Chapter

New Animals

Besides looking for living fossils and strange animals that people claim to have seen, cryptozoologists have identified new animals. One of the first discovered was the okapi. It was found in Africa in 1901. African people described it as a cross between a giraffe and a zebra. Scientists say the okapi is the closest living relative to giraffes.

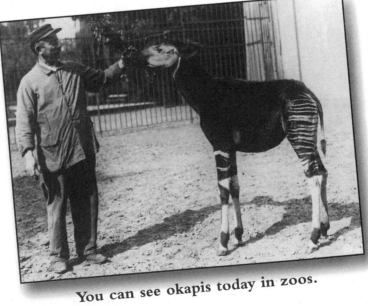

You can see okapis today in zoos.

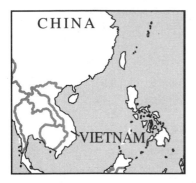

Many of the most recent large animal discoveries have come from the forests of Vietnam and the jungles of Paraguay. These are two places that have remained largely unexplored by scientists.

One of these new animals is the kouprey (KOO pray). The kouprey is a large wild ox native to parts of Vietnam. It was discovered in 1937, when a kouprey was brought to a French zoo. The zoo director claimed it was a new animal, but no one believed him.

Vietnam is also home to two other kinds of wild oxen, the gaur (gawr), and the banteng (BAHN teng). Zoologists believed the kouprey was not a new animal at all, but some kind of animal that was part gaur and part banteng.

In 1961, a detailed study proved that the kouprey was different. It is so different from the area's other wild oxen, in fact, that it was placed in an entirely new classification, or group, of animals.

Soon after the kouprey was accepted as a genuinely new animal, Vietnam entered into a long period when it was at war. Many kouprey were killed in the fighting. The kouprey is now an endangered species. There are only a few dozen that continue to survive in the wild.

Unfortunately, the kouprey's ability to hide may not help it to survive. In 1988, a team of Vietnamese zoologists began a program to capture koupreys so they could be bred in captivity. Then the species would be saved. The koupreys managed to avoid capture. The team was finally forced to give up.

In the 1970s, after the war in Vietnam was over, zoologists began exploring the forests again, looking for other new animals. They succeeded when they found the saola (sow la). It was in the same area as the kouprey.

The saola is another oxlike creature that has horns and long teeth, big eyes, and a fluffy tail. It is the largest new land animal found since the kouprey.

A saola

A Chacoan peccary

In Paraguay, a country in South America, small wild pigs called peccaries have been known for a long time. However, a special kind of peccary, called the Chacoan (CHAH koh un) peccary, was thought to have been extinct since prehistoric times.

The Chacoan peccary has a longer snout, ears, and legs, and a shorter tail than other peccaries. Natives of Paraguay described it as a "donkey-pig." A biologist named Ralph Wetzel went to Paraguay in 1974. He discovered that this donkey-pig really was a Chacoan peccary.

Like other peccaries, the Chacoan peccary sleeps during the day and is active only at night. Perhaps this is why the Chacoan peccary had remained hidden from zoologists for so long.

Cryptozoology makes exciting advances when zoologists identify what looks like a mix of two animals as something entirely different. It also makes advances when scientists really listen to people's stories about unusual animals.

Hidden Fact

Vietnam promises to be a rich area for new animal discoveries in the future. Since the saola was found, scientists have discovered two new bird species, a new fish, a tortoise, and two other mammals.

Chapter

Working Together

Bernard Heuvelmans has said that cryptozoology would not be possible without people who are curious and determined to search for the unknown. Cryptozoology would not be possible without the help of many other kinds of scientists as well as ordinary people.

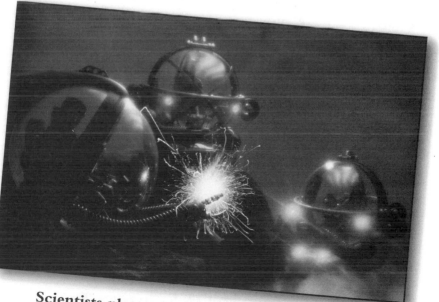

Scientists plan to use this Deep Rover in 2001 to search underwater for the giant squid.

With underwater lights, scientists searched Loch Ness for Nessie in 1976.

Biologists and zoologists are needed to help cryptozoologists correctly identify new creatures. Paleontology, the study of fossil remains, has also been a big part of cryptozoology. Stories that people have told for years about unusual creatures are also important. They keep alive important information about animals that would otherwise remain unknown.

The kraken was a creature in stories until scientists discovered that it really existed. Perhaps some day cryptozoologists will be able to tell for sure whether Bigfoot or Nessie are real animals.

44

Scientists have learned one thing from the discovery of new animals such as the Chacoan peccary. They have learned the importance of keeping an open mind. Just because something sounds impossible doesn't mean it isn't true.

Ralph Wetzel kept an open mind when he heard stories about an animal he thought might be the Chacoan peccary. If he had not gone looking for proof that the stories were real, this animal would have been lost to science.

Professor Smith never gave up on the coelacanth even though it ended up taking almost 20 years. Until he found a second coelacanth, many zoologists believed his find to be a very ordinary fish called the grouper.

A coelacanth

Like many cryptozoologists, Professor Smith believed for many years that the coelacanth had survived. Then, when he finally found one, he could not prove it was real because the animal was not complete. However, he didn't give up. Finally, his patience was rewarded.

Today more and more scientists are entering the field of cryptozoology. They are traveling to new places and listening to the stories people tell.

A cryptozoologist listens to the story of a South American man.

Cryptozoology is also becoming more familiar to many people. Articles on hidden animals can be found in magazines. Shows on television treat hidden animals as real possibilities. Now that you know about cryptozoology, you may want to learn the stories of other hidden animals.

Hidden Fact

Who knows what fascinating creatures cryptozoologists will find next? For instance, some people say that the saber-toothed tiger, long believed to be extinct, still lives in Paraguay.

Glossary

classified   [KLAS uh fyd] sorted or arranged in groups

expeditions   [eks puh DIHSH unz] trips for some special purpose such as exploration or scientific study

extinct   [eks TIHNKT] no longer alive; all members of a group having died out

eyewitness   [eye WIHT nus] person who sees or has seen some event or thing and can describe it

investigations   [ihn vest uh GAY shunz] careful searches; detailed examinations

prehistoric   [pree hihs TOR ihk] before recorded history, such as in the time of the dinosaurs

preserved   [pruh ZURVD] kept from harm or change

research   [REE surch] a careful hunting for facts or truth about a subject

species   [SPEE sheez] group of related organisms that are the same in certain ways and are able to breed or have babies with each other

tentacles   [TEN tah kulz] group of long, slender flexible growths around the head or mouth of an animal, usually used to hold, touch, or move